Engineering Elephants

Emily M. Hunt, Ph.D.
and
Michelle L. Pantoya, Ph.D.

AuthorHouse™
1663 Liberty Drive
Bloomington, IN 47403
www.authorhouse.com
Phone: 1-800-839-8640

First published by AuthorHouse 3/29/2010

ISBN: 978-1-4490-5816-6 (sc)

Library of Congress Control Number: 2010903523

Printed in the United States of America
Bloomington, Indiana

authorHOUSE®

To all the inspiring minds that will engineer our future…

Engineers make elephants
with long, swinging trunks
Wait a minute...

Do engineers really make elephants?
No, but they do make roller coasters!

Up and down, around again
Roller coasters are so much fun!
Engineers design the loops
Sometimes two…or just one!

Momentum holds you in your seat
And keeps the car on the right path
Engineers make it all work
Using science and math!

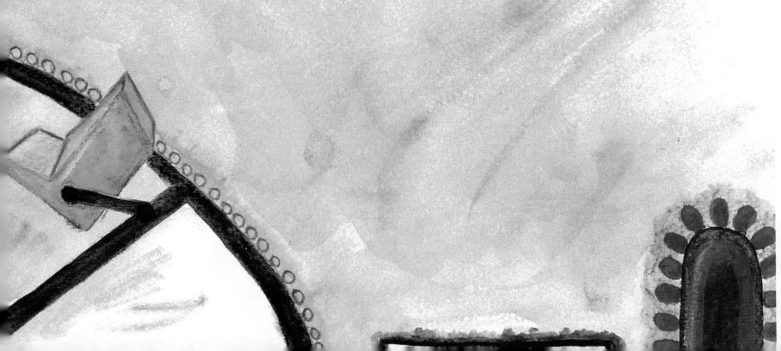

Engineers make
volcanoes
hot lava bursting
from within

Wait a minute...

Do engineers really
make volcanoes?
No, but they do
make race cars!

Zoom, Zoom, Zoom!
race cars whirl around the track
using gasoline to go faster,
always trying to lead the pack!

There are forces that slow down the cars
The worst of these is drag
Race cars designed by engineers
are first at the checkered flag!

Engineers make eggs
with thin, fragile shells

Wait a minute...

Do engineers really make eggs?

No, but they do make surf boards!

In the big blue ocean filled with waves
A surfer rides along the water's ledge
Sun in the sky, beach in sight
On a board engineered to push the edge!

The surfer stands, ready to go
Using the water to float the ride
Surfs up, dude! He shouts out loud
As aerodynamics enhance his glide!

Engineers make ladybugs
Small and red with dots

Wait a minute…

Do engineers really make ladybugs?
No, but they do make helper hands!

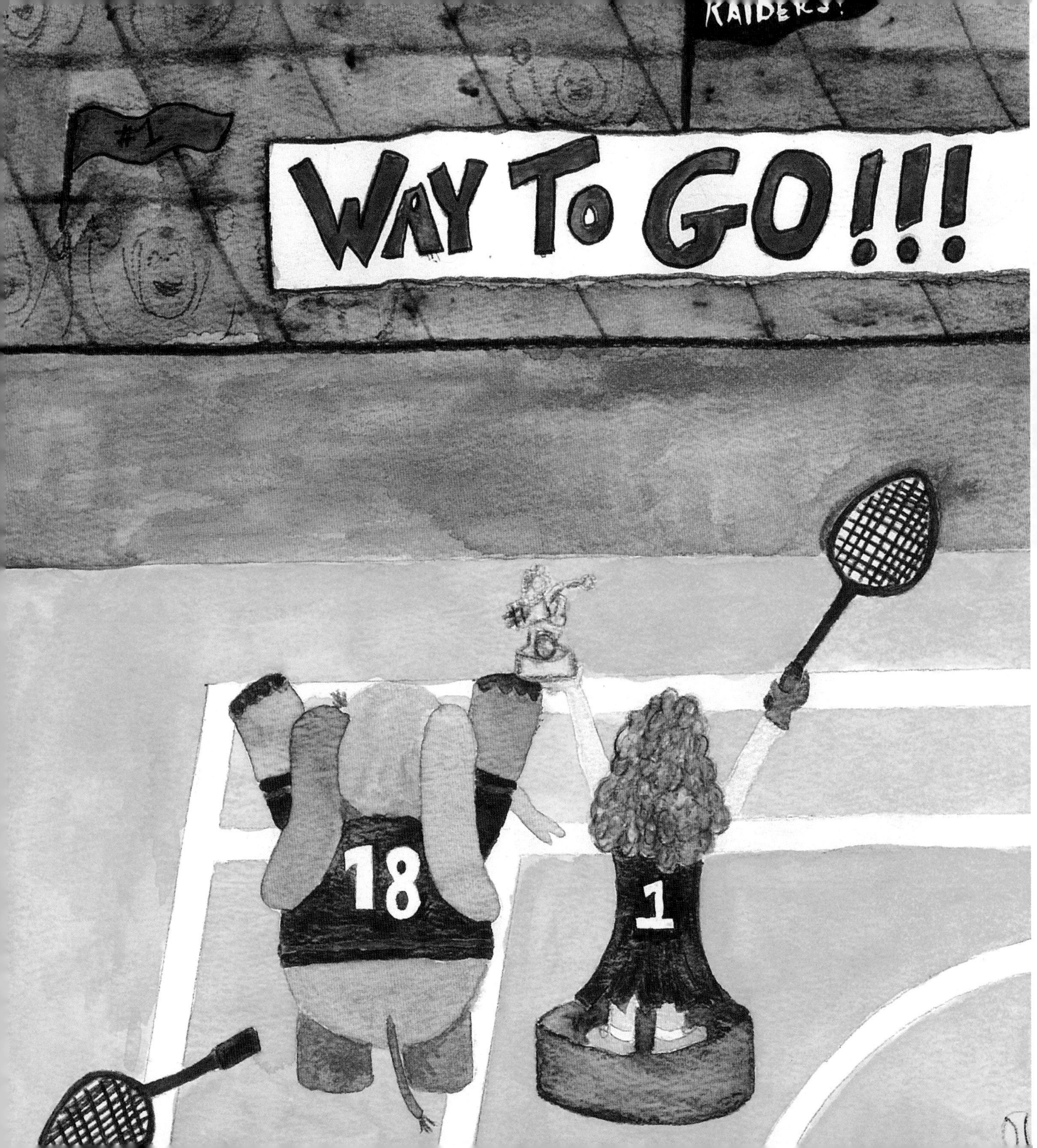

RAIDERS!
#1
WAY TO GO!!!
18
1

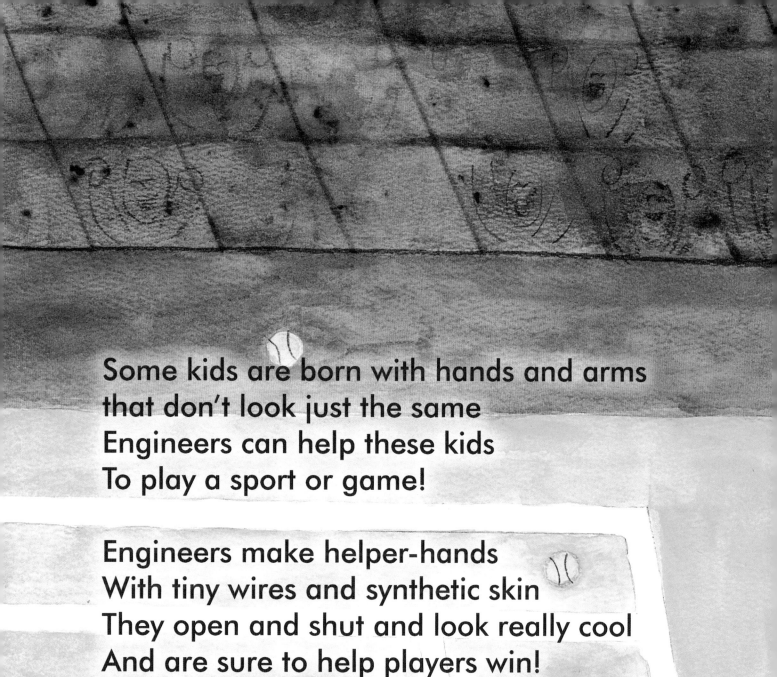

Some kids are born with hands and arms
that don't look just the same
Engineers can help these kids
To play a sport or game!

Engineers make helper-hands
With tiny wires and synthetic skin
They open and shut and look really cool
And are sure to help players win!

Engineers make clouds
heavy and dark with rain

Wait a minute...

Do engineers really make clouds?
No, but they do make energy!

A new way for producing energy
Built on top of country hills
Wind turns them round and round
Turbines that look like wind mills!

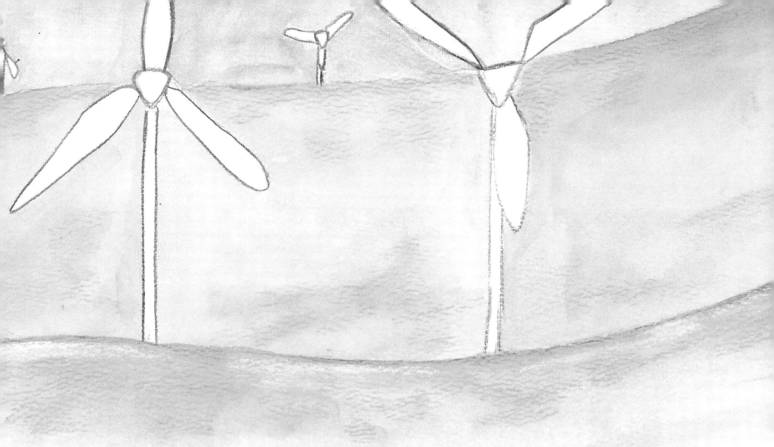

Engineers design them big and tall
To make electricity for power
The blades are a special material and shape
To produce lights and heat at any hour!

Engineers make trees
Fresh and green and rough

Wait a minute...
Do engineers really make trees?
No, but they do make new
materials!

Composite materials are used for a bicycle
To make it lightweight and easy to load
Shiny as silver and strong as steel
A bike engineered for the road!

Football helmets are made from plastic
Its molecules forming one long chain
Engineered to absorb the impact
To protect the player from any pain!

Engineers make bats
Black and mysterious and blind

Wait a minute...

Do engineers really make bats?
No, but they do make fireworks!

Bang, boom,
crackle, pop!
Engineers know how
to combine
The right chemicals
into fireworks
To make the night
sky shine!

The mixture is started with a blast
An explosion occurs in the air
Look up high at the beautiful colors
A fireworks show for us all to share!

Engineers make rainbows
Red, yellow, and green

Wait a minute...

Do engineers really
make rainbows?
No, but they do make
rocket ships!

A rocket ship is made for flight
And can sail around the stars
The ship moves faster and faster
Circling Earth and heading toward Mars!

As the ship moves through the sky
It uses gas and solid fuels
Engineers put the ship in space
Math and science are the tools!

Engineers make toes
Big and little and stinky

Wait a minute...

Do engineers really make toes?

No, but they do make new fabrics!

Kids keep warm with heat from the sun
But soon the cold north wind blows in
The temperature drops as heat starts to transfer
It feels too cold on the skin!

Engineers design new fabrics
Making cloth with little strings called nano threads
These materials keep kids warm and dry
In scarves and hats to protect little heads!

We have learned that engineers design roller coasters, race cars, surf boards, helper hands, wind turbines, composites, fireworks, rocket ships, and new materials...

When you grow up to be an engineer, what new things will you create?

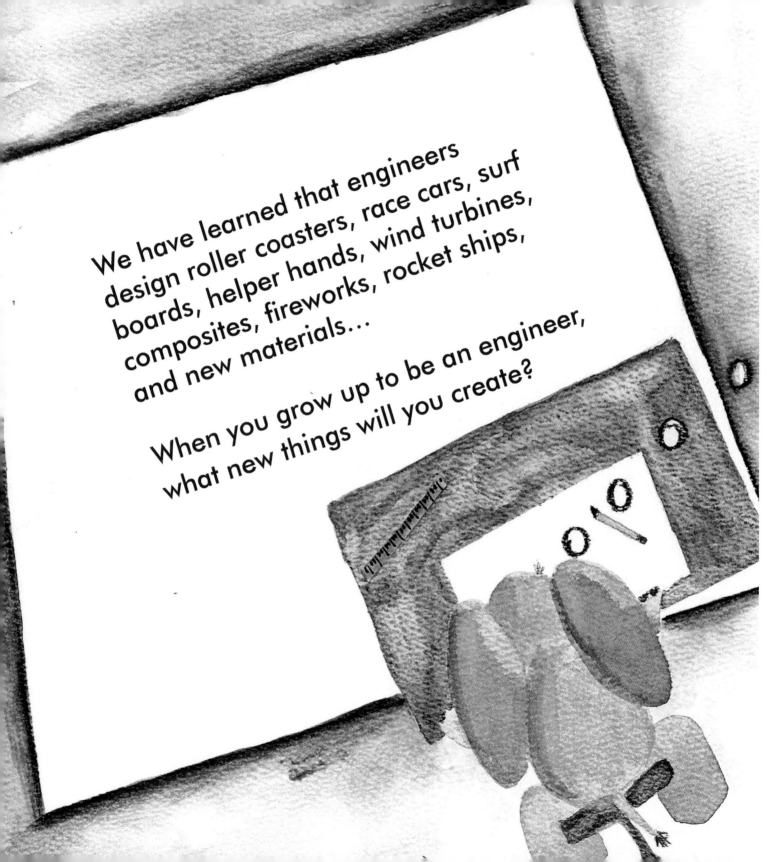

22629726R00024

Made in the USA
Lexington, KY
06 May 2013